Colour Dublin

GREGORY AND AUDREY BRACKEN, from County Kildare, are a brother and sister with a love of travel. They have published guides to cities such as London, Paris, Hong Kong and Singapore with total sales of more than 20,000 copies. Gregory teaches Architecture at the Technical University of Delft in the Netherlands. After a career in publishing and marketing in London and New York, Audrey now lives and works in Dublin. They are authors of the popular *Dublin Strolls* architectural guidebook.

Stay up-to-date with the authors at:

www.gregory-bracken.com

www.facebook.com/DublinStrolls

www.instagram.com/dublinstrolls

Dedicated to our brother Gary,
who has shared in many adventures (travel and otherwise)
over the years, with hopefully many more to come.

Faience roundel on Sunlight Chambers, corner of Essex Quay and Parliament Street.

Colour Dublin

Gregory and Audrey Bracken

The Collins Press

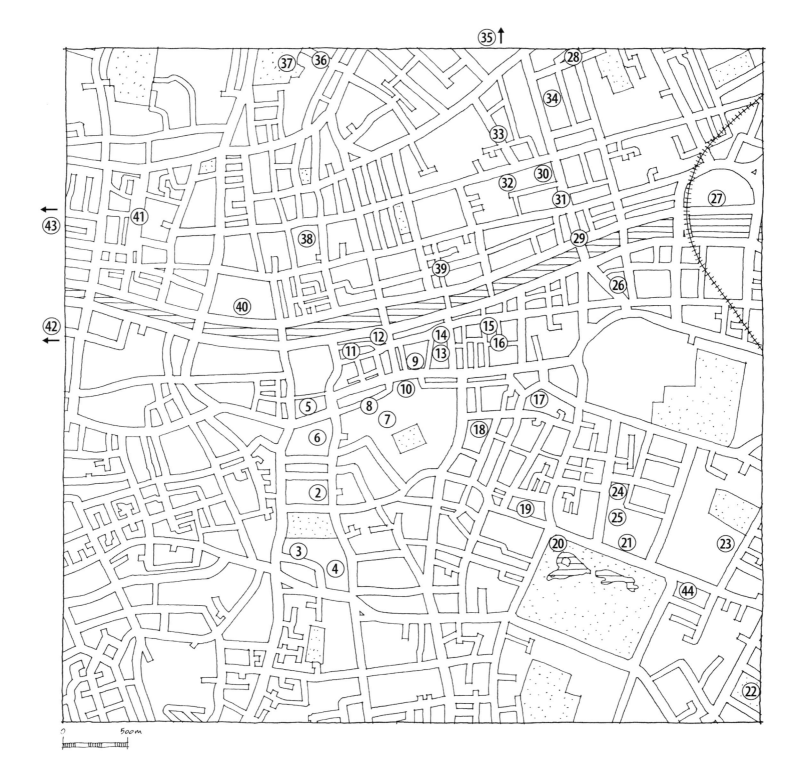

Contents

Introduction

Dublin is a beautiful city, with gracious streets and squares, world-famous theatres and magnificent museums. Vikings founded the city in 841. It was a useful stop on their way to the Mediterranean and it rapidly became one of the largest settlements outside Scandinavia. The area around Dublin Castle is thought to have been inhabited as far back as 7500 BC, and there was a later influx of Neolithic farmers and herdsmen in the fourth millennium BC. Celts began to arrive around 700 BC, and by the time St Patrick arrived in AD 432 they were happy to embrace Christianity. A golden age followed, with churches and monasteries being built, including St Patrick's Cathedral, where St Patrick baptised his converts.

The name Dublin derives from the 'black pool' (*dubh linn* in Irish), which lay behind Dublin Castle (and is now covered by Castle Garden). This was the confluence of the Liffey and Poddle Rivers (the latter is now culverted, but it used to run around the Castle). The Irish name for Dublin was and is *Baile Átha Cliath* ('ford of the hurdle') and refers to a crossing on the River Liffey near Fr Mathew Bridge. When the Anglo-Normans invaded in 1169 they put their mark on the city. Dublin grew into an important and prosperous place, protected by its defensive walls. And this is the era when the great cathedrals of Christ Church and St Patrick's took on the shape we see today.

By the eighteenth century Dublin had begun to burst its medieval seams. The city flourished in the Georgian era, becoming an aristocratic capital ruled by an enlightened Protestant elite known as the Ascendancy. It was they who founded the Wide Streets Commission in 1757. Established to oversee the expansion of the city, it produced gracious new streets and bridges, including O'Connell Street and Bridge (originally Sackville Street and Carlisle Bridge). Speculative development (often by the same men on the Commission) produced elegant residential squares. This is also when some of the most beautiful buildings in the city were built, including the Neoclassical Custom House and the Four Courts. Dublin was at this time one of the largest and richest cities in Europe but the Act of Union in 1801 brought this golden era to a close. The Irish parliament was dissolved and many aristocrats and businessmen (often one and the same) decamped to London. The city entered a decline that lasted (particularly for some parts of the north side) until the second half of the twentieth century. Dublin's aristocratic character turned decidedly commercial in the nineteenth century and this had an effect on its architecture, which tended to be showier; it was certainly less gracious. The country also had something of a rollercoaster ride, from the elation of Catholic Emancipation in 1829 to the misery of the Great Famine in the 1840s, not to mention numerous rebellions and their brutal suppressions.

The rebellion that led to independence (after seven centuries of British rule) took place in Easter Week 1916 when a handful of freedom fighters took over some of the city's key buildings. The General Post

Office (GPO) was the headquarters and was where the Irish Republic was proclaimed. The British, shaken to the core, and fearful that it would prove a dangerous distraction in their fight against Germany in the First World War, overreacted. They flattened O'Connell Street and surrounding areas, then rounded up and shot the rebel leaders at Kilmainham Gaol. Public opinion, which had not, initially, been particularly in support of the Rising quickly swung in its favour – exactly what the rebels had hoped for when they planned their 'blood sacrifice'.

Once the First World War was over Ireland proclaimed its own parliament in 1919 and a brief War of Independence ensued. This ended with the 1922 Treaty partitioning the country into a 26-county Free State (with the King of England still King of Ireland) and six counties of Ulster staying in the United Kingdom. This led to a civil war (and stored up troubles for Northern Ireland which exploded in the 1960s). After the Civil War, Ireland found the going tough; there was the Depression of the 1930s, an economic war with England at the same time and then the Second World War (although Ireland remained neutral). This was reflected in the city, which became greyer, with parts of it even becoming derelict. Those who could afford to do so moved to the suburbs.

Ireland became a full republic in 1948 but it was not until the 1960s that the country began to experience any degree of prosperity, and this was relatively short-lived. It was only in the 1990s that the city, and the country, saw the beginning of a more sustained era of wealth and well-being. Long-dead parts of the city began to liven up and people began to move back into the centre. Places like Temple Bar exemplified this new spirit: a spontaneous urban regeneration that got government support.

Urban regeneration was one of the most visible signs of what came to be known as the Celtic Tiger – a remarkable period of economic boom. Sadly this energetic and overexcitable beast suddenly and quite unexpectedly expired in 2008, but before it did so it managed to claw the overinflated property bubble, plunging the country, and particularly Dublin, into a financial crisis from which it took a long time to recover (although the Irish tend to be good in a crisis; it is success we cannot seem to handle). One of the best legacies of the late twentieth-century boom was, however, the fact that a lot of the city's derelict sites were filled in, and some of the more thoughtful regeneration projects, like the Docklands, stayed vital and interesting throughout.

1

Dublin Coat of Arms

Dublin was granted a coat of arms in 1607 and it can be seen all over the city on public buildings and even on many of the decorative lamp posts. The crest depicts three burning castles on a blue background. Blue was St Patrick's colour and traditionally associated with Ireland until green took over in the nineteenth century when it became identified with the cause of Irish freedom. The castles may not be castles at all: some think they may be Viking gates (Dublin was founded by the Vikings in 841). The fact that each of them is burning is probably meant to represent Dubliners' fervour in protecting their city. The motto under the coat of arms reads '*Obedientia civium urbis felicitas*'. Latin for 'Obedient citizens; happy city', this is a sentiment that the British rulers would no doubt have approved of.

2

Iveagh Play Centre

Designed by McDonnell and Reid, this was the most ambitious school building in the city when it was built in 1913. A jaunty, jolly red-brick building with Portland stone dressing, it works particularly well with St Patrick's Park (which was probably designed by the same firm). The whole ensemble has the feel of a handsome country house, especially its Edwardian interpretation of the Queen Anne style. Two storeys over basement, the entrance front has a tall gable, as do the ends. The central two-storey bay window is flanked by giant Ionic pilasters, while the gabled ends have single-storey bay windows with similar paired giant orders. The building's plan is simple and rather institutional, but this is appropriate given that it is still used as a school.

3

St Patrick's Cathedral

Ireland's largest cathedral, and the national cathedral of the Church of Ireland, it was founded at a well where St Patrick is supposed to have converted Irish people to Christianity in the mid-fifth century. Built in the 1220s in the Early Gothic style, it replaced a wooden chapel dating from the tenth century. The tower was built by Archbishop Minot between 1363 and 1375 but it collapsed in 1394 and was rebuilt around 1400. The granite spire was added in 1749. Comprehensively restored by the Guinness family in the 1860s, the fine stained-glass windows date from this time. Jonathan Swift was Dean of the cathedral from 1713 to 1745.

4

Marsh's Library

This is the oldest public library in Ireland. Built for Archbishop Narcissus Marsh, it was designed by William Robinson and built from 1701 to 1703. It was extended by Thomas Burgh in 1710 when a library wing and entrance porch were added. A plain building with modest decoration, it was extensively rebuilt by the Guinnesses in 1863 when a new entrance front and stair hall were added. The interior remains intact, however, and is one of the most charming in the city with wired-off alcoves where readers were locked in with their books.

5

Christit Church Cathedral

This cathedral was commissioned by Strongbow (the Anglo-Norman conqueror of Dublin) and Archbishop Laurence O'Toole in 1172. It replaced an earlier, wooden structure founded around 1030 by King Sitriuc. The oldest parts of it date to the end of the twelfth century. Originally a monastery, complete with cloister, it was built in the Romanesque style. The monastery was dissolved by Henry VIII in the 1530s and Christ Church became a secular cathedral. The cloister buildings were used as law courts until the Four Courts were built in 1796. Almost completely rebuilt in 1868 by George Edmund Street in a high Victorian style, it is now one of the best examples of Gothic Revival architecture in the country.

6

Leo Burdock's

This is Dublin's oldest and most famous fish-and-chip shop. It was founded by Leo Burdock in 1913 and was still using coal to heat the frying pans as late as the 1990s, the last chip shop in the country (and probably the world) to do so. Popular with tourists and locals alike, it really is a Dublin institution. You can see the queues snaking their way up Werburgh Street each evening as people wait to get their hands on the delicious golden-fried fish. And as the saying goes, you can see everyone here, from the street sweepers all the way down to politicians.

7

Record Tower, Dublin Castle

King John (of Magna Carta fame) ordered a fortress built in Dublin in 1204 and a large rectangular structure was erected at the southeast corner of the old city. It had four circular towers and a moat filled by the River Poddle. For 700 years it represented English rule yet, oddly, it was only seriously attacked once, when Silken Thomas laid siege as part of his unsuccessful rebellion against Henry VIII in 1534. The Record Tower is the most complete part of the medieval castle. Also known as the Wardrobe Tower, it dates from the 1220s and was restored by Francis Johnston between 1810 and 1813.

8

Bedford Tower, Dublin Castle

Dublin Castle became the viceregal residence in 1560 and underwent expansion in the sixteenth and seventeenth centuries. Following a bad fire in 1684, William Robinson laid out the Upper and Lower Yards as you see them today. The Bedford Tower, also known as the Guard House, was begun in 1750 and completed in 1761. This elegant building, with its octagonal tower topped by a cupola, was further altered between 1776 and the 1820s and is, architecturally speaking, one of the best buildings in the entire castle complex.

9

Olympia Theatre

A much-loved Dublin institution, its plain exterior masks a gem of a Victorian interior. Built in 1879, when it was known as the Star of Erin Music Hall, it was remodelled in 1897 when it became the elaborate Rococo confection we see today. Renamed the Empire Theatre at the time, this was changed to the Olympia following Ireland's independence in 1922. The theatre was beautifully restored in 1980 but the iconic cast-iron glass canopy over its entrance was knocked down by a lorry in 2004; it has since been rebuilt.

10

City Hall

This Neoclassical masterpiece sits on a hill facing down Parliament Street. Designed by Thomas Cooley (who won the international competition), it was built between 1769 and 1779 as the Royal Exchange but was taken over by Dublin Corporation in 1851 and became City Hall the following year. The building has three formal facades, including one facing up the rather narrow Castle Street, but this street used to be a major thoroughfare before Lord Edward Street was laid out in the nineteenth century. Held by rebels during the 1916 Easter Rising, the building's façade is still scarred by bullet holes.

BRACKEN JAN '06

11

Smock Alley Theatre

This charming theatre was originally built as the church of Ss Michael and John and dates from 1811–13. It was designed by John Taylor in a Gothic style and has a prettily gabled granite façade with Tudor-style pointed windows and a centrally placed clock. It incorporates the old Theatre Royal, originally opened in 1662 and the first Theatre Royal outside London. Plays premiered here include Richard Brinsley Sheridan's *School for Scandal* and Oliver Goldsmith's *She Stoops to Conquer*. David Garrick also first performed his Hamlet here. It was used as a whiskey store until Fr Michael Blake bought the building and had the church built. This closed down in 1989 and the building has since been sensitively converted once again into a theatre.

12

Sunlight Chambers

On the corner of Essex Quay and Parliament Street sits this delightfully quirky building completed in 1901 for soap makers Lever Brothers. Its four storeys are decorated in a colourful and light-hearted Victorian reinterpretation of fifteenth-century Italian architecture. The two strips of faience panelling between the storeys depict the production and use of soap in the Renaissance.

BRACKEN JAN '06

13

Meeting House Square

This pleasant little piazza was created when the Temple Bar area was revamped in the 1990s. The square hosts open-air screenings of film, theatre and music which are free, but you need to get tickets from the Temple Bar Information Centre in advance. There is also a food market every Saturday with outstanding local Irish organic produce.

14

The Ark

The Ark is a purpose-built cultural centre for children housed in a former Quaker Meeting House. Originally built in the 1720s, and substantially remodelled in 1877, this handsome symmetrical six-bay palazzo-type façade was retained when the complex was converted in the 1990s. The rear of the building houses the stage that faces onto Meeting House Square.

BRACKEN FEB '06

15

Temple Bar Square

This narrow north-facing square is home to cafes, shops, galleries and bars and is popular with people lounging on the long steps on its north side to watch the world go by. Temple Bar Gallery and Studios faces onto the square, a mid-1990s street-front gallery and artists' studios on a large irregular site, while next door to it is the Black Church Print Studio, an artistic collective with studio facilities and a shop selling members' artwork.

16

Crown Alley

The gentle slope of Crown Alley still contains a two-storey mid-twentieth-century factory building which was converted into a restaurant in the 1980s and is a rare glimpse of the sort of architecture typical of Temple Bar before it got revamped in the 1990s. The rest of this popular cobbled street is home to shops and cafés, and looming over it is the Central Bank, a 1970s monster designed by Stephenson Gibney and Partners which faces onto Dame Street. A large building, with a somewhat overstated structure, it has gradually wormed its way into Dubliners' affections over the years.

17

Church of St Andrew

This former Church of Ireland place of worship has been home to the Dublin Tourism Office since 1996. The building itself dates from the 1860s and is a lovely Gothic-style building that replaced a much-rebuilt structure from 1670. An ambitious and skilfully designed plan, it seems a little too large for its cramped site. There is a lovely cloister-like walkway along St Andrew Street but cost-cutting during construction meant that some of the planned ornaments never got added (the central buttress of the cloister contains a large lump of unfinished stone, and the niche above it is empty).

18

George's Street Arcade

Also known as the South City Markets, this delightful red-brick Victorian Gothic market hall, complete with corner turrets, was built by Lockwood and Mawson between 1878 and 1881 after winning the competition. It occupies the entire city block between South Great George's Street and Drury Street and is supposed to be the oldest shopping centre in Europe. After a bad fire in 1892 W. H. Byrne was asked to rebuild. He removed the market hall and inserted rows of brick-fronted shops. These have lovely timber-and-glass roofs supported by cast-iron brackets and are popular for second-hand clothes, old books and records, as well as antique jewellery and other assorted bric-à-brac.

19

Gaiety Theatre

This lively yellow-brick Italian Gothic building dates from 1871. Its lavishly decorated three-tier Victorian Rococo auditorium has hosted everything from grand opera to pantomime. Deemed obsolete in 1954, luckily it was saved from demolition, refurbished and given a new lease of life. Refurbished again in 2003, it continues to be one of the city's most popular entertainment venues. The pavement in front of it has handprints of Irish celebrities under a new glass canopy popular with buskers. The handsome red-brick buildings adjoining it to the east, numbers 51–54, were built around 1910 and still contain their original shopfronts.

20

Fusiliers' Arch

The Grafton Street entrance to St Stephen's Green is graced by an elegant Neoclassical triumphal archway which dates from 1907 and was built to commemorate Irish soldiers killed in the Boer War (earning it the nickname 'Traitors' Gate'). Designed by J. Howard Pentland for the Office of Public Works, its handsome granite arch is flanked by four rusticated piers that curve to create an effective forecourt. The names of various battles are inscribed around the top, while all those who died are remembered in lists on the arch's underside.

21

Shelbourne Hotel

This iconic Dublin institution was founded by Martin Burke in 1824. The last of Dublin's grand nineteenth-century hotels, it has recently been beautifully refurbished. Originally designed by John McCurdy in 1865, this five-storey, ten-bay, red-brick building is enlivened by its elaborate plasterwork, as well as the massive two-storey bay windows that flank its entrance. The entrance canopy, which was added later, is a particularly fine piece of wrought-ironwork, while the four torch-bearing statues – two Egyptian princesses and their shackled Nubian slaves – are Dublin icons.

22

Fitzwilliam Square

Completed in 1825, this is the smallest and last of Dublin's great Georgian squares to be built and the only one that still has a central garden open only to resident key-holders. Developed by Richard, seventh Viscount Fitzwilliam (who also developed nearby Merrion Square), it was designed in 1789 and began to be laid out from 1792. The centre was only enclosed in 1813 (thanks to an Act of Parliament in Westminster) and some of the leases (on the south side) only became available for building in the 1820s. Famous residents have included the artist Jack B. Yeats (who lived at number 18).

23

Government Buildings

The last major building project by the British in Ireland, it was supposed to house new government departments and the Royal College of Science. Designed by Aston Webb (also responsible for Buckingham Palace) and Thomas Deane, it was built between 1904 and 1922 and is a vast Portland stone palace arranged around a courtyard. The dome and entrance portico line up with the main entrance, which consists of a screen of columns topped by urns and statues of Irish scientists. The Irish government took over the building in 1922 and it is now home to the Department of the Taoiseach (Prime Minister).

24

St Ann's

This Church of Ireland place of worship was founded in 1707 and the first church built here in 1719. The current building's handsome Italian Romanesque facade was added by Deane and Woodward in 1868. The tall gable is flanked by towers; the broader of the two, to the north, was never completed (it should have had a belfry). The stone is granite and limestone with Portland stone and red sandstone dressings and there is some lovely nineteenth- and early twentieth-century stained glass. The Vicarage, to the south, is a nineteenth-century addition to an eighteenth-century rectory and is also by Deane in a style similar to the church.

25

Mansion House

Set back overlooking a cobbled forecourt off Dawson Street is Dublin's Mansion House, the official residence of the Lord Mayor, a function it has had since 1715 when Dublin Corporation bought the five-year-old house from its owner, Joshua Dawson. This delightful Queen Anne building is the oldest free-standing house in the city. Originally of brick, it was rendered in 1851 and the characteristically decorative iron porch was added in 1886.

Bracken Feb 15

26

Bord Gáis, Hawkins Street

This half-timbered Tudor-style building is actually the rear of the Art Deco Bord Gáis former showrooms on D'Olier Street (and you can get a hint of their style by the sign's lettering). This is where the boardroom is located, a sober wood-panelled room overlooking this narrow little street that runs down to the River Liffey. Hawkins Street was home to the Theatre Royal, three of them, in fact, mostly built in Neoclassical style, although the last incarnation, from 1935, was an elegant Art Deco. Sadly, this was demolished in the 1960s to make way for Hawkins House, an insensitive office complex considered one of the ugliest buildings in the city.

GA

BRACKEN JAN '06

27

Custom House

James Gandon's masterpiece dates from 1791 and has to be considered one of the most elegant government buildings ever constructed. Gandon's first large-scale commission, it is arguably Dublin's most accomplished Neoclassical building, as well as one of its largest. Consisting of three two-storey blocks forming an H parallel to the river, the riverfront block is entirely clad in creamy Portland stone and has a domed central portico linked to end pavilions by arcades. The carvings are by Dublin sculptor Edward Smyth, with the keystones representing Ireland's rivers and the Atlantic Ocean. Damaged by the IRA in 1921, who tried to burn it down, it was rebuilt in 1926 and refurbished in the 1980s. It is now home to the Department of the Environment.

28

Ss George and Thomas

This charming Italian Romanesque-style Church of Ireland place of worship was built by Frederick Hicks in 1931. He won the Royal Institute of Architects of Ireland (RIAI) Gold Medal for its design. It replaces a much larger church by John Smyth dating from 1758–62, which was the focal point of the long vista down Sean McDermott (originally Gloucester) Street. This is a delightful little building with an arcaded porch at the west end and a simple bell tower that would not look out of place in a small town in Tuscany. The wheel-shaped window is filled with bottle-green glass.

29

O'Connell Street and Bridge

O'Connell Bridge was built in 1876–80 to replace James Gandon's original Carlisle Bridge (which dated from 1791–95). It was the first bridge downstream of the old medieval city. The O'Connell Monument is one of the finest monuments in the city. Designed by John Henry Foley, it was begun in 1866 but only completed in 1883. You can see bullet holes in the statues dating from the 1916 Easter Rising. O'Connell Street is just over 600 metres (nearly 2,000 feet) long and 46 metres (150 feet) wide and consists of two roadways, one on either side of a central monument-lined walkway. Originally called Sackville Street, the 1916 Rising left the street in ruins. It was rapidly rebuilt in the 1920s, and a sense of unity was achieved thanks to the uniform building height, cornice level and Neoclassical detailing.

30

General Post Office

This is a large grey three-storey granite building with a Portland stone fluted Ionic portico sticking out over the pavement. When it was completed in 1818 the General Post Office, or GPO as it is more popularly known, was a symbol of modernity; a century later it took on a new significance: as the birthplace of the Irish Republic. Originally built by Francis Johnston, it was remodelled between 1904 and 1915 and then all but destroyed during the Rising – all that was left was a burnt-out shell. It was completely rebuilt during the 1920s.

31

Eason Bookshop

This popular bookshop is housed in a building dating from 1919. Designed by J. A. Ruthven, this whole part of O'Connell Street had to be rebuilt after it was destroyed in the 1916 Easter Rising. It is a handsome three-bay edifice housing five storeys of books. Apparently, during the Rising, when rebels were being rounded up from a nearby pub, one of those arrested included an Eason's delivery driver who had nipped in for a quick pint after his shift.

32

GPO Arcade

This covered arcade runs from Henry Street to Princes Street North and was part of the General Post Office designed by Francis Johnston and opened in 1818. Almost totally destroyed during the Easter Rising in 1916, it was reconstructed between 1924 and 1929, with the arcade itself being designed by P. J. Munden and built in 1928–29. This new arcade almost doubled the size of Johnston's original and consists of a wide central passageway under a glass roof supported by slim arches. It is home to a number of shops and cafes with Ionic columns and some Postmodern detailing on the railings at mezzanine level.

BRACKEN FEB '15

33

Moore Street

Running between Henry Street and Parnell Street, Moore Street is one of the city centre's best and liveliest street markets and specialises in fruit, vegetable and flowers. Hearing the stall holders shout their wares is like being transported back to an earlier era. Laid out in the early eighteenth century, it was substantially damaged during the 1916 Easter Rising. In fact, it was in the back room of a poultry shop at number 16 that the members of the Provisional Government decided to surrender. Named after the Moore family, who were Earls of Drogheda, the street still has some lovely original shopfronts.

34

Gresham Hotel

Founded at numbers 21 to 22 O'Connell Street Upper in 1817 (when this part of the street was known as Sackville Street), this famous hotel was later extended to include number 20. It survived the Easter Rising unscathed but was then occupied by anti-Treaty forces during the War of Independence and destroyed by government troops. Rebuilt between 1925 and 1927 to designs by Robert Atkinson, its large Portland-stone elevation consists of eleven bays with a ground-floor row of Ionic pilasters framing large arched windows and a decorative glass canopy over its three-arched entrance. A balcony runs across the first-floor windows linking the shallow projecting blocks at either end, which are topped by carved sphinxes.

35

Garden of Remembrance

This narrow but lovely city park marks the spot where some of the leaders of the 1916 Easter Rising were held before being taken to Kilmainham Gaol (where nearly all of them were shot). Dedicated to the memory of those who died for Irish freedom, it was opened in 1966 to mark the fiftieth anniversary of the Rising. A long cross-shaped pool features a mosaic depicting broken swords, shields and spears to symbolise peace and leads the eye to the large sculpture called *The Children of Lir* by Oisín Kelly.

BRACKEN FEB '15

36

Henrietta Street

Named after Henrietta, Duchess of Bolton (wife of an eighteenth-century Lord Lieutenant), this is the finest early Georgian street in Dublin. The street, which runs up a low hill, was laid out by Luke Gardiner. The houses are grand, maybe even a little grim, with their huge brick elevations unadorned except for an occasional and somewhat sober doorcase. Though the street itself had little influence on the planning of the rest of the city, this plain style exerted a huge influence on homes in Dublin for the next century. Originally bounded by open fields at the top, the street now terminates in the triumphal arch that leads to King's Inns. Almost the entire north side of the street was sold in the 1890s and fell into tenements. Some brave souls have been painstakingly restoring these mansions since the 1970s.

37

King's Inns

The Lawyers' Society of Ireland changed its name to King's Inns when Henry VIII declared himself King of Ireland in the 1530s. By the early eighteenth century their old premises on the site of the Four Courts was in bad shape so James Gandon was asked to design new Inns where barristers could live and study. Construction of this symmetrical Neoclassical building with cupola started in 1800 but funding was soon curtailed and plans for the new plaza on Constitution Hill was scrapped. Gandon resigned from the project in frustration in 1804 and Francis Johnston took over, completing it in 1817. He also added the archway onto Henrietta Street in 1820.

38

City Markets

Officially known as the City Fruit and Vegetable Wholesale Market, these large covered markets were designed by Parke Neville (who died in 1886) and built by his successor, City Engineer Spencer Harty, in 1891–92. Consisting of eight iron-and-glass ranges surrounded by an arcaded wall of red and yellow brick, the wall above the arches consists of terracotta tiles sporting fish, fruit and vegetables. The main entrances are on Mary's Lane and Arran Street West and boast tall arches flanked by twinned Corinthian columns – the Mary's Lane entrance has a sculptural group (by C. W. Harrison) representing Fair Trade and Justice on either side of a shield featuring Dublin's coat of arms.

39

Swift's Row

Swift's Row sits at the heart of a warren of new streets nestling on the north side of the Liffey and linked to Temple Bar via the Millennium Bridge, an elegant pedestrian bridge opened in 2000. This area has become a veritable Little Italy in recent years and is home to a wonderful variety of restaurants, bars and cafés to suit every taste and price range.

40

The Four Courts

Designed by James Gandon and built between 1786 and 1802. A geometrically complex plan crowned by a landmark dome, it is a robust and muscular building. Gandon arranged the courts in an X with a vast empty circle at the centre. The dome over this vast space was his masterstroke. Based on the Pantheon in Rome, it is an unmissable part of the city skyline. Sitting on a base of Corinthian columns it has a diameter of just over 20 metres (about 50 feet). The huge niches on either side of the portico now contain windows, added during the 1932 reconstruction – the building had been badly damaged during the Civil War.

BRACKEN JAN '06

41

Smithfield

Smithfield was laid out as a livestock market in the 1660s. Some old houses still survive, mostly from the late eighteenth and early nineteenth centuries, at the northern end. By the nineteenth century the area had become quite industrial, and famous for distilling. Most of the east side was taken over by Jameson's whiskey. This huge space was revamped in 1997 and has begun to be an interesting place to go out in the city.

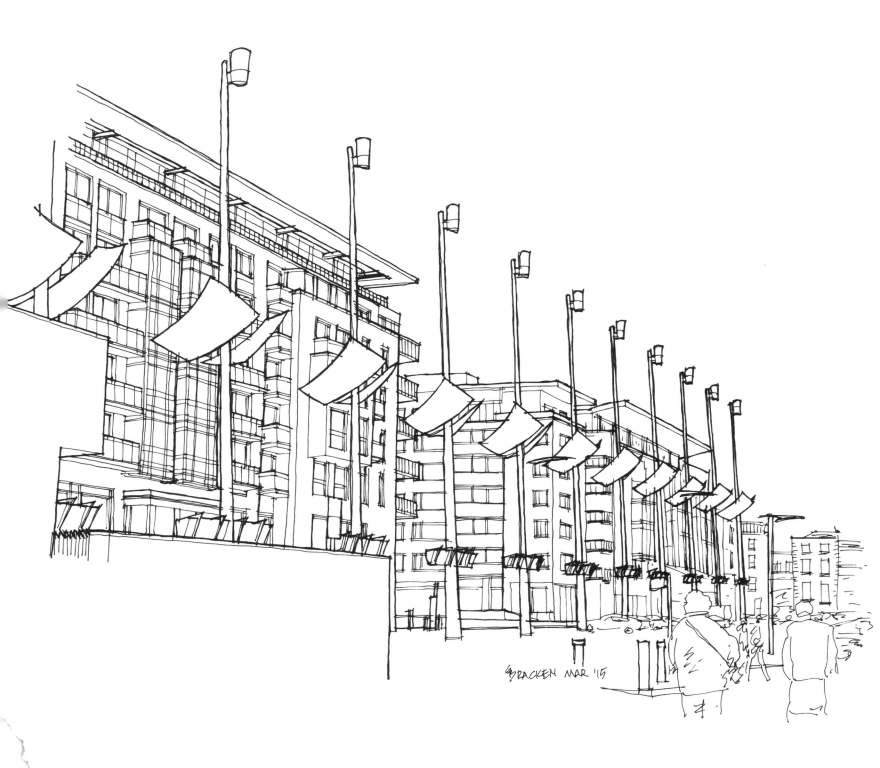

BRACKEN MAR '15

42

Guinness Brewery

Home to Ireland's most famous export, and Dublin's most popular tourist destination, the Guinness Brewery was founded in 1759. Proximity to the city reservoir and the Grand Canal and River Liffey, combined with the famous recipe for stout (a type of porter), meant that the company saw prodigious growth throughout the nineteenth and twentieth centuries. It became the largest brewery in the world by the early twentieth century (and it is still the largest in Europe). This is the largest industrial complex in the city centre with a site covering 26 hectares (65 acres). The enormous concrete silos overlooking Victoria Quay are a landmark on the city's skyline.

43

Ashtown Castle

Ashtown Castle is a small limestone tower house dating from the 1590s. It became home to one of the Phoenix Park keepers in the 1660s and was upgraded to residence of the Park Ranger a century later. It was the colonial Under-Secretary's residence from 1785 and, after independence, Ashtown Lodge, as it was known, became the Papal Nunciature with a chapel being added in 1930. It was abandoned in 1979 and the Office of Public Works demolished all the later additions in 1986 to reveal the original tower house. They turned the stable yard into the attractive Phoenix Park Visitors' Centre and the layout of the vanished house can still be seen in the low box hedges beside the tower.

44

Shopfront, Merrion Row

Merrion Row is a small, narrow street linking busy Baggot Street to the north-east corner of St Stephen's Green. About halfway down the south side sits this lovely, light-hearted Neoclassical commercial building dating from the end of the nineteenth century. It graces a street so busy that few people even notice they are walking under a rather fine oriel window cantilevered over the pavement from the centre of the first floor. This sits neatly over the middle of three Georgian-style wooden-arched windows that form the tastefully decorated shopfront, making this a gem of Victorian architecture.

First published in 2017 by
The Collins Press
West Link Park
Doughcloyne
Wilton
Cork
T12 N5EF
Ireland

A CIP record for this book is available from the British Library.

Paperback ISBN: 978-1-84889-316-0

Typesetting by Carrigboy Typesetting Services
Typeset in Chaparral Pro
Printed in Malta by Gutenberg Press Limited

Georgian Terrace